I am Different, I am Me.
Bedtime Healing Meditation for Children

Little Blue Zen

I am Different, I am Me.
Copyright@ 2024 Jo Galloway

The right of the author has been asserted to her following the copyright writing, designs and patent act of Australia.
All rights reserved. No part of this book may be reproduced, stored or transmitted by any means whether auditory, graphic, mechanical, or electronic without the written permission of the author. Unauthorised reproduction of any part of this work is illegal and is punishable by law.
Unless otherwise noted, the author and the publisher make no explicit guarantees as the accuracy of the information contained in this book may differ based on individual experiences and context
ISBN: 978-1-7635801-3-8

Published by Little Blue Zen
Birdwood NSW
Printed in Australia
Cover Design: Gagan Karunachandra
Editing: Kristine Gibson
jo@littlebluezen.com
http://www.littlebluezen.com

I am Different, I am Me.

Bedtime Healing Meditation for Children

Jo Galloway

Your child may like other books in this series

- Bully Proof. Keeping out the bullies.

- A Coat of Flying Colours. Passing your Exams.

- The Magical Treasure Hunt. Building Confidence.

- The Magical Worry Balloon.

- Angelic Dreams. Meet your Guardian Angel.

- Scared of the Dark.

- I Love School.

- Bedwetting. Dry Nights.

Little Blue Zen.com

INTRODUCTION

Why Healing Meditations.

As children we make sense of our experiences based on our limited understanding and perception. We may misinterpret events or draw conclusions that form the basis of limiting beliefs that influence our entire life. These beliefs become ingrained over time, shaping our thoughts, feelings and behaviours well into adulthood unless consciously challenged.

In my work as a practising Hypnotherapist, I've found that all my clients' concerns, whether rooted in fears, feelings of inadequacy, addictive behaviours, or other challenges, trace back to their early childhood experiences, interactions, and upbringing. It's important to note that these issues don't exclusively stem from abusive or dysfunctional environments; limiting beliefs can arise from various circumstances.

Parents or caregivers wield substantial influence in shaping our perceptions of ourselves and the world around us. Remarks, criticisms, or comparisons made by family members can foster beliefs about our capabilities, worthiness, or potential. Furthermore, interactions with peers, teachers, and authority figures also contribute to the formation of these beliefs. Repeated experiences of rejection or failure can solidify beliefs such as "I'm not good enough" or "I'm unworthy of love."

This realization ignited my passion for intervening at the source: working with children to prevent these beliefs from taking root and manifesting into significant challenges in adulthood. By addressing issues early on, we can guide children to develop into the best versions of themselves, free from the burden of limiting beliefs that could otherwise dominate their lives.

.

How Healing Meditation will help your child.

Teaching children meditation offers a multitude of benefits that can positively influence their daily lives and overall development. A regular mindfulness meditation practice provides valuable tools for managing stress, navigating emotions, and promoting overall well-being. Healing meditations, in particular, bolster your child's self-belief, helping to remove any resistance they may face in adulthood. This leads to a happier, more successful and fulfilling life.

Unlike traditional meditation, which often centres on relaxation, healing meditations go a step further by focusing on recovery, balance, and reprogramming a child's self-belief. These meditations use techniques such as breathing exercises, visualization, and guided imagery to not only foster deep relaxation but also reshape their mindset.

This targeted approach helps build a stronger sense of self-confidence and resilience. By integrating positive affirmations and emotional healing, healing meditations offer a distinct advantage over traditional methods, laying a powerful foundation for a child's future success and well-being.

Meditation can also be an effective part of your child's bedtime routine, helping to calm the mind and prepare the body for restful sleep. Techniques like guided imagery and deep breathing, as outlined in this book, can signal to the brain that it's time to wind down.

Sharing these calming moments at bedtime not only strengthens the bond between parent and child, but also creates a supportive and nurturing environment. It also sets a positive example, emphasizing the importance of self-care and mindfulness.

With patience and consistency, you can help your child develop a lifelong practice that supports their mental, emotional, and physical health. Give your child the gift of relaxation and imagination with this easy-to-read story designed to inspire and uplift.

I am Different, I am Me.

We are all created differently, each one of us unique. Embracing our differences is a wonderful thing. "I Am Different, I Am Me," is a special bedtime story that highlights the importance of being unique and special while inspiring children to feel a sense of belonging, build confidence in themselves and appreciate their own talents.

Your child's special friend will captivate them with a magical tale about stars. Through this enchanting story, each child realizes their own uniqueness and extraordinary nature, much like the stars in the sky. This empowering story encourages them to embrace their individuality and appreciate their special gifts.

This heartwarming tale aims to empower your child, fostering confidence in their unique talents and helping them discover the joy of embracing their true selves.

I AM DIFFERENT * 5

Give your child the gift of imagination and relaxation at bedtime with this easy-to-read story. It begins gently, helping your child relax and become open to the positive messages woven throughout the tale.

This soothing meditation gently lulls your child to sleep while planting positive suggestions in their subconscious mind. Children have incredible imaginations and absorb these suggestions easily, which can lead to significant positive changes in their lives.

This story helps them address inner worries that may be behind difficult or unusual behaviour's, fostering a sense of security, happiness, and self-confidence.

Delivered in a slow, monotone voice, this story captivates and soothes. I AM DIFFERENT, I AM ME, is also available on YouTube, providing a soothing auditory experience children can enjoy at home, in the car, or anywhere they need a moment of relaxation."

Listen on YouTube

6 * I AM DIFFERENT

I am Different, I am Me.

It's bedtime, my beautiful Starlight.

Climb on in and snuggle up.

We are about to go on a wonderful adventure.

But first, let's take a nice big, long stretch.

Stretch out your whole body, from the top of your head down to the tips of your toes.

Have a little wriggle, too.

When you are ready, lying nice and still, softly close your eyes.

Wonderful.

Now, take a deep breath in through your nose.

Feel your tummy rise as you breathe in.

Now, slowly breathe out through your nose and feel your tummy go down.

Good job!

Let's do that again.

Take a deep breath in, pushing your tummy up and out.

Now, breathe out slowly as your tummy goes down.

Perfect!

Let's do it one more time.

Take a deep breath in, as big as you can.
Now, breathe out slowly, imagining you're a balloon gently letting out all its air.
Great job!
Feel your body getting floppy and light.
Feel yourself sinking down into your soft, cozy bed.
Let all your muscles relax completely.
Doesn't that feel so nice?
It's wonderful to feel sleepy and cozy as you settle into your comfy bed.
Imagine yourself floating down, down, down, drifting away peacefully.

The sleepy feeling can start anywhere you like.

Maybe it begins at the top of your head, slowly moving down your body, all the way to the tips of your toes.

Or is it the other way around for you?

Do your feet get warm first?

Then the comfortable, sleepy feeling spreads all the way up to the top of your head.

Maybe the sleepy feeling spreads out from the middle of your tummy?

You now feel comfortable on the inside and comfortable on the outside.

You are laying very still now.

If someone were to look at you they would think you were sound asleep.

Your legs are all floppy, your arms are all floppy too.

Your head is sinking down into your beautiful soft pillow.

Your eyelids are so heavy now that it is impossible to open your eyes.

They are glued shut, sealed shut and locked tight.

Did you know you can see perfectly well even with your eyes closed?

That's because children have the most wonderful imaginations, even better than grown-ups.

Let's imagine you're playing in a very special park.

The sun is shining brightly, warming your skin on this wonderful sunny day.

You can hear the birds singing cheerfully in the trees above.

Best of all, you're playing with your favourite special friend.

Your most favourite person in the whole wide world.

You know exactly who this special friend is.

Your special friend places a soft fluffy picnic rug on the green grass beneath a big old fig tree.

They kindly invite you to sit down on the soft rug.

Your special friend would like to tell you a magical story.

An incredibly special story.

Feeling a little sleepy, you sit down and cross your legs, feeling the warmth of the sun on your shoulders.

Now your friend shares their story with you.

You know this is a special story because someone wrote it just for you.

They whisper softly and you lean in to listen.

Did you know that when God made the universe and created all the little boys and girls, he placed a star in the night sky for every child born?

When you look up into the night sky, you can see a million, maybe trillions of dazzling, sparkling stars.

Every child's star is different, a different size, a different colour, even a different shape.

Some stars shine brightly, while others just flicker.

Some stars are shy, hiding behind other stars.

Each star is different, magical, and special in their own cosmic way.

Just like all the boys and girls in the world.

No two stars are alike, no two are the same.

Do you know which star belongs to you?

You were not created to be like every other boy or girl, just as no star is identical to another in the sky.

You were not created to be the same as your parents or the same as your friends.

Not even the same as your brothers or sisters.

We were all created to be different.

You can never be exactly like them, because you are you, I am me, and that is the way it is meant to be.

Being different is a good thing, right?

Imagine how dull the world would be if we were all alike?

What could we learn if we all liked the same things, and all played the same games?

What if everyone wanted to bat the ball, but no one wanted to pitch or throw the ball?

That would be no fun at all.

Your special friend explains we cannot all be good at the same things.

Some of us are awesome at sports, while some of us are good at math.

But hey, that's okay.

Some of us are good at drawing, while some of us have a way with animals.

But guess what? That's okay too.

Because I am me, you are you, and that is exactly how it is meant to be.

We are all blessed with our own special design.

God made each of us different, with our very own special gifts.

You might think, I am not good at sports, but I love to cook!

Or maybe, cooking isn't your thing, but wow, can you sing?

We all have our very own special gifts to share with the world.

Your special friend tells you that your star shines the brightest when you are doing what you love.

That is when your heart feels like it is singing because you are so happy.

Whether it is reading, swimming, playing or even building things, your special gift is unique to you.

It's okay to be different, because you are you, and I am me.

That is the way it is supposed to be.

Did you know there is no one else in the world exactly like you?

That means you are incredibly special.

You can feel proud of who you are, just being yourself.

A very special child.

You make friends easily because everyone can see how dazzling you are.

You love sharing your special gifts.

You are amazing just the way you are!

Notice how happy you feel showing everyone just how extraordinarily clever you are.

Think about all the things that you love to do.

What makes you the happiest?

Remember, you are special; you are loveable, and you are good enough.

You are the brightest star in the night sky.

When you are happy, everyone around you feels happy too.

Now that you know how special and clever you truly are, you can feel calm and happy.

You feel confident wherever you go and whoever you are with.

You know all the special things about yourself.

It is okay to be different, just as you are you and I am me.

That is the way it is meant to be.

Every child has something amazing to share with the world.

That is why we are all born differently.

We all look different, enjoy different things and even like different foods to eat.

I love oysters, but do you?

Everyone has their own likes, talents and special qualities.

Think of some of your friends.
Can you spot their special gifts?
What makes them different from you?
What makes their star shine bright?
Maybe they like something you don't?
They might like one thing, but you like another.
But hey that's okay, because you are you and they are them.
That is the way it is supposed to be.
Every day you remind yourself: I am different because I am me, I am not you.
I am me, and that is exactly how I was born to be.

I enjoy being me.

I like how I look.

I like how I think.

I enjoy what I do.

I am me, not you, and that's just the way I like it.

You love being different.

Being different makes you feel special because you are unique.

You are one of a kind, incredibly special.

Stand tall and feel proud of who you are.

You are you, and that is exactly who you're meant to be.

Now, light up the sky, and let your star shine brightly for everyone to see.

Be the brightest star in the universe.

You're here to be yourself and do the best job you can.

So, next time you look up into the night sky, see your star shining the brightest for the entire world to see.

You are happy, confident and special, just the way you are.

Knowing this and believing in yourself is really important.

Next time you look in the mirror, you tell yourself just how special you truly are.

Feeling so happy, it is now time to say goodnight to your special friend, and gently, peacefully drift off to sleep.

Tonight, you will dream the most magical dreams.

In the morning, you will wake up feeling happy, knowing deep within just how special you truly are.

Because you are you, I am me and that is perfectly okay.

That is just the way it is supposed to be.

So, good night, my little Starlight.

Sweet Dreams..........

Also by Jo Galloway

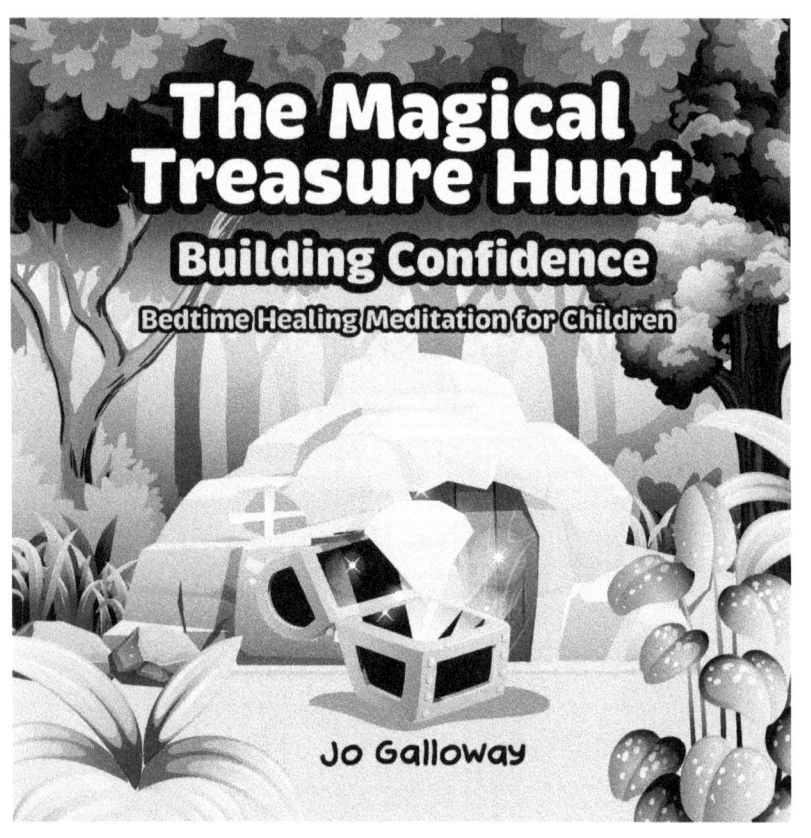

Embark on a whimsical journey with your little one as they venture into the world of self-discovery. As you guide your child through a series of relaxation exercises, they'll descend a rainbow staircase to meet their most cherished friend. Together they travel along an enchanted path. Here they'll uncover glittering stones inscribed with powerful messages: "I am lovable," "My body is beautiful just as it is," "I am good enough," and "I am confident." Each stone is a reminder of their unique strengths and worth, helping them embrace their true selves and shine with self-love and confidence.

A Coat of Flying Colours

Jo Galloway

Sitting exams can often bring to the surface a child's self-sabotaging beliefs of I am not good enough, fears of failure or fear of rejection, along with bucket loads of anxiety.

Wearing the magical coat of Flying Colours is like wearing Superman's cape. This coat will transform your child's inner beliefs, allow access to their phenomenal memory, and enable them to remain calm and in total control while undertaking any exam.

Allow this gentle healing meditation to ease their worries, enhance their belief in their capabilities, empower their positivity to pass every exam with flying colours.

www.ingramcontent.com/pod-product-compliance
Lightning Source LLC
Chambersburg PA
CBHW042356070526
44585CB00028B/2949